D1757886

LITTLE BOOK OF

BEETLE

Jon Stroud

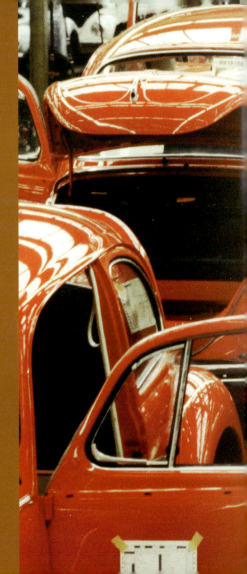

LITTLE BOOK OF

BEETLE

First published in the UK in 2010

© G2 Entertainment Limited 2013

www.G2ent.co.uk

All rights reserved. No part of this work may be reproduced or utilised in any form or by any means, electronic or mechanical, including photocopying, recording or by any information storage and retrieval system, without prior written permission of the publisher.

Printed and bound in China.

ISBN 978-1-907803-05-5

The views in this book are those of the author but they are general views only and readers are urged to consult the relevant and qualified specialist for individual advice in particular situations. G2 Entertainment Limited hereby exclude all liability to the extent permitted by law of any errors or omissions in this book and for any loss, damage or expense (whether direct or indirect) suffered by a third party relying on any information contained in this book.

All our best endeavours have been made to secure copyright clearance for every photograph used but in the event of any copyright owner being overlooked please go to www.G2ent.co.uk where you will find all relevant contact information.

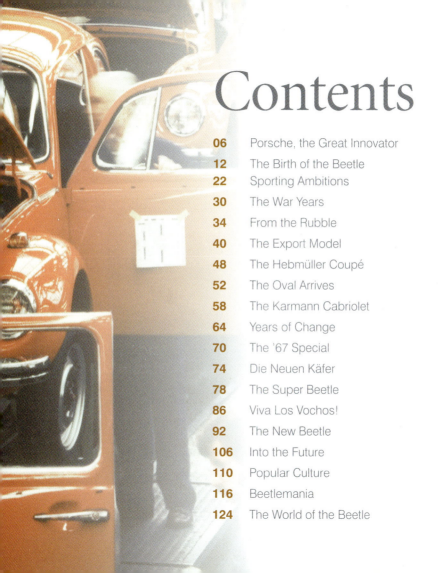

Contents

LITTLE BOOK OF **BEETLE**

Porsche, the Great Innovator

RIGHT Henry Ford's Model T – motoring for the masses

While the friendly looking Volkswagen Beetle is, in modern times, associated with feelings of fun, frivolity and freedom, its origins date from far different times and one of the darkest of chapters in 20th century world history.

In the wake of the First World War, Germany had found itself in a state of near permanent bankruptcy – saddled, as it was, with the unwelcome prospect of having to repay some 226 billion Reichsmark (RM) (£11.3 billion)of war reparation to its enemies of old. Cars were seen as an absolute luxury and far beyond the means of all but the most well-heeled and wealthy of the Fatherland's aristocrats and industrialists. This was in stark contrast to the goings on 4,000 miles to the west in the United States of America.

Motoring pioneer Henry Ford famously declared that "nothing is hard if you divide it into small jobs" – a philosophy he admirably demonstrated when, in 1913, he introduced the world's first conveyor belt assembly line to his Highland Park factory and in doing so reduced the time taken to produce a single Model T from well over 12 hours to a mere 93 minutes. A manufacturing revelation, this innovation at last freed the automobile from its elitist stranglehold and brought it within the financial grasp of the working man. In 1909, a standard Model T cost $850 but, with the advent of automated production, this soon fell to below $500 and, within 10 years, the Tin Lizzy was priced at just $290.

International acknowledgement of Ford's remarkable achievement seemed to know no bounds. His greatest fan was, however, also his most unlikely – a

former army corporal, polemicist and would-be politician called Adolf Hitler. Such was his level of admiration, Hitler even went to the lengths of hanging a portrait of the American industrialist upon his office wall. For the dictator in waiting, a nation mobilised by the automobile was a dream he was determined to see brought to fruition.

Adolf Hitler's opportunity to realise *Motorisierung*, the motorisation of Germany, finally came in 1933 after his appointment as Chancellor when, in his first formal appearance, he addressed an audience consisting of the nation's chief automobile executives assembled for the Berlin Motor Show. "We must have a real car for the German people," he demanded; "simple, reliable, economic." It was to be capable of carrying a family

of four and cost less than 1,000 Marks, bringing it within the financial grasp of anybody who could afford a motorcycle.

Although not present at the 1933 meeting, another person, one with somewhat less politically radical views, shared Adolf Hitler's vision for a car of the people – a *volks wagen*.

The son of a tinsmith and born in the North Bohemian village of Maffersdorf (now part of the city of Liberec in the Czech Republic), Ferdinand Porsche had carved quite a reputation for himself as an innovative engineer.

Having displayed a prodigious aptitude for electrical and mechanical engineering at a very young age, he studied part time at the Imperial Technical School in Liberec before taking a job as a student employee with Vienna-based Béla Egger Electrical shortly after his 18th birthday. It was during his time here that the youthful Porsche developed an electric wheel hub motor – a design so far ahead of its time that it is only now, over a century later, that its true potential in automotive design is finally being realised.

After moving to a new post at luxury coachbuilders Jacob Lohner Werke

und Sohn in 1898, his new employers were quick to capitalise on this new technology and the System Lohner-Porsche – a car powered by electric motors fitted within the front wheel hubs – was born. With no cumbersome drivetrain to cause power-sapping friction, the Porsche hub-drive system operated with an extraordinary level of efficiency (a staggering 85%). It was, however, sadly held back by the arcane battery technology of the day, requiring 1,800 kg of lead acid batteries to provide sufficient power.

Undeterred, Porsche took his design idea a step further with the even more innovative *Mixte* system, which abandoned the vehicle's weighty battery system in favour of a more efficient (and lightweight) diesel power plant to provide power for the electrical hub system and to charge a much smaller on-board battery pack. Sound familiar? Yes, Ferdinand Porsche had developed the world's first hybrid car.

Porsche's engineering genius soon attracted interest from bigger players in the burgeoning automotive industry. In 1906, at 31 years old, he was recruited by Austro-Daimler as their head of

RIGHT The Type
32, built for NSU
– already the
Beetle's famous
profile is starting
to take shape

design and within 10 years held the post
of managing director. It was here that
he first touted the idea of following in
Ford's footsteps in producing a small,
lightweight and less expensive car for
the masses, but it was to no avail.
Despite his heady position within the
company he failed to garner the support
he needed to push the concept forward.
Porsche finally left Austro-Daimler
in 1923 after a series of tempestuous
arguments regarding the future direction
of the company's car development.

Within a couple of months he
had a new position – this time with
the Stuttgart-based *Daimler-Motoren-
Gesellschaft* (DMG) – and a new role as
technical director. After the company's
merger with Benz & Cie to form
Daimler-Benz, Porsche put his technical
know-how towards producing some
of the greatest racing cars of the era,
culminating in the legendary and
dominating Mercedes-Benz SSK. Once
more he petitioned his employers to
investigate the possibilities of producing
a small car but, again, their interests lay
elsewhere and his ideas were dismissed.

Finally, in 1930, frustrated by their
lack of vision and the restrictions

imposed when working for the larger
automotive companies, Ferdinand
Porsche decided that it was time to
create his own wholly independent
design and engineering consultancy.
Having recruited a small but highly
skilled team of engineers, aerodynamicists
and manufacturing specialists, Porsche
soon learned that the Nürnberg-based
motorcycle manufacturer Zündapp were
keen to introduce a small, practical car
to its popular range. Porsche's initial
design for the company, the Type 12,
incorporated his new torsion car rear
suspension (a simple and inexpensive
system which replaced traditional coil
springs with a tube filled with metal rods)
and a four-cylinder air-cooled engine.

Zündapp were keen to utilise this
new suspension system but not the
engine – preferring instead to use
a heavy, water-cooled five-cylinder
radial motor instead. The Zündapp
manufactured *Volksauto* prototype,
was, however, something of a disaster
– its engine overheated, its gearbox
disintegrated and the torsion bar
suspension system, manufactured from
low-grade steel, shattered. Admitting
defeat, Zündapp reverted to two-

wheeled manufacture instead of four.

In 1932, Porsche took his ideas to NSU – a company which had started life as a knitting machine manufacturer but had been a producer of motorcycles and cars since the turn of the century. Company owner Fritz von Falkenhayn had also expressed a desire to add a small, affordable car to his range and agreed to Porsche's suggested use of a rear-mounted, air-cooled engine, torsion bar rear suspension system, as well as to a new rounded Porsche-designed body which, with the gift of hindsight, was clearly a premonition of the most famous car in motoring history. But, for a second time in succession, the design was never to be realised further than the prototype stage, after a deal to sell the company's car business to Italian manufacturer Fiat made any further progression impossible.

The Birth of the Beetle

When Adolf Hitler outlined his dream for a people's car, he knew exactly what he was looking for: first and foremost, the vehicle was to be capable of carrying a family of five in comfort at a speed of around 80 km/h. Furthermore, it was to be powered by an air-cooled engine to enable it to be started with ease during the harsh German winters and to combat overheating on long, hot winding Alpine climbs in the summer months. It was also to cost no more than 1,000 RM (about 35 weeks' wages for the average working man).

Jakob Werlin held an enviable position within Hitler's administration – the Mercedes-Benz representative, having established himself a role as the Führer's key advisor on all matters automotive. Werlin, with his finger pressed firmly on the pulse of the German car industry, was certainly the man for the task. He was more than aware of Porsche's work for Zündapp and NSU and his ongoing interest in the development of a small

33
A.H.

car for the masses, so decided to pay an unannounced visit to Porsche's Stuttgart consultancy. With the seeds of hope planted, Porsche began to formulate his ideas.

Finally, on 17 January 1934, Dr Ing. h.c. Ferdinand Porsche published his "Exposé" for the design of a future "German Volkswagen". It may well have been early days but, in effect, the Beetle had been born.

Porsche's work was, as one would expect, concise, considered and of the greatest detail. Accompanied by a series of sketches, his designs incorporated his trademark torsion bar suspension and, of course, a rear-mounted flat-four air-cooled engine. But key to his proposal was the idea that a small, efficient car for the people should not be, as he described it, a "pantograph solution" with artificially scaled down dimensions, output and weight. By contrast, his people's car was to be

ABOVE Adolf Hitler's very own interpretation of a "people's car"

BELOW Hitler
views a model
Volkswagen
with delight

RIGHT Ferry
Porsche behind
the wheel of a
Volkswagen V2
prototype, 1935

capable of competing with any other car on equal terms.

Weighing in at 650 kg, it could carry a family of four in comfort – not at the Führer's prescribed 80 km/h but at a speedy 100 km/h – and, with its efficient 25 horsepower 1250cc engine running at around 3,500 rpm, would return a healthy 30 miles per gallon without putting any components under undue stress or strain.

The greatest challenge for Ferdinand Porsche was in meeting Hitler's demand for a 1,000 RM price limit. By any stretch of the imagination this was a

tall order, and one which had been the stumbling block for many a design in the past. But if there was one thing that set Porsche aside from other designers, it was his ability to innovate and rise to a challenge. His torsion bar suspension was cheap to produce and effective in use, as was the concept of using a rear-mounted air-cooled motor – its positioning eliminated the need for a weighty and inefficient drive shaft and its construction did away with the requirement for a radiator, fan and pump.

During the 1934 Berlin Motor Show, Porsche was summoned to Hitler's suite at the Kaiserhof Hotel to present his ideas. Hitler was soon contributing with sketches and ideas of his own, and in May of that year famously commented that the shape of the car should resemble a beetle.

Eager to please their leader, the *Reichsverband der Deutschen Automobilindustrie* (RDA), an organisation comprising the nation's leading car manufacturers including Auto Union, BMW and Daimler-Benz, finally signed a contract with Porsche to develop a prototype Volkswagen *on their behalf* in the summer of 1934. However,

the matter of who might actually build such a car should it come to fruition was still left unanswered.

Work soon commenced on what was to become the first Volkswagen prototype – the V1. Easily recognisable as the forerunner to the Beetle we know and love, its design was beautiful in its simplicity. There were, however, some striking differences visible in this early test machine. The lights, rather than being set into wings, sat proud on the bonnet like the eyes of a bug and there was no rear window – instead, the back of the car was dressed only by a series of horizontal cooling slats above the engine bay. The floor, rather than being made of steel or aluminium was, in fact, constructed of plywood.

Nevertheless, in December of 1935, Ferdinand Porsche himself drove the fledgling V1 from his Stuttgart offices to Munich to demonstrate his progress to Adolf Hitler. The meeting had been set up by the project's catalyst, Jakob Werlin, who was obviously angling for a senior position in the management of the Volkswagen and had been keeping the Führer informed of the car's development on a weekly basis.

Unfortunately for Werlin and Porsche, neither of them had taken the time to inform the RDA of their intention to show off the new machine.

The RDA was incandescent with rage. Deeply suspicious of all around them, the motor industry felt thoroughly aggrieved that some Bohemian car designer, however technically brilliant he might be, had seemingly gone behind their backs. After all, it was with the RDA and not the Führer that Porsche had signed his contract. In a top secret document circulated within the industry, the RDA

rallied against Porsche with its chairman, Dr Robert Allmers, criticising the whole project and Porsche in particular. Porsche subsequently demonstrated the V1 and the V2, its convertible co-star, to the RDA in February of 1936.

While the design was impressive and progress was being made in many ways, there was one respect in which the Volkswagen still lagged far behind

– its engine. Early in its development, the V1 was fitted with a double-piston two-stroke designated the A-Motor (A60). Although the original test engine was only 850cc in capacity (a 1000cc unit having been promised), it soon became apparent that, in addition to overheating issues, the design was never going to be capable of generating enough low-end torque. An alternative was sought in the D-Motor (D60) – a four-stroke overhead valve (OHV) flat twin. But, even before reaching the prototype stage, speculative calculations suggested that it would be incapable of reaching the specification demanded of Porsche's Exposé. At best it would have an anticipated top speed of 80 km/h but would never be powerful enough to cope with the steep gradients of Germany's Alpine south.

A new engine was needed and the task of designing it was handed over to a young, talented Austrian engineer by the name of Franz Xaver Reimspiess. Like Porsche himself, Reimspiess was a perfectionist, an innovator and a man capable of impressive lateral thinking. Within just days of being entrusted with this important assignment, he had already come up with the basic construction that would be used in the Beetle for the next 50 years.

Designated the E-Motor, its *boxer* format (a configuration in which opposing pistons move in and out simultaneously rather than in alternation) utilised a bore of 70mm and a stroke of 65mm. This "over-square" design was in contrast to other mass

production engines of the time where the convention was to run a stroke longer than the bore of the piston. Reimspiess's ingenious shorter-stroke design required the pistons to do far less work and, therefore, be capable of allowing the engine to run at maximum revolutions for longer periods of time without fear of overheating and causing less general wear and tear on components. Also new to the industry was the idea of constructing the entire engine from a light alloy – this was a material usually reserved for high-end designs and not for mass production.

At the same time, a new series of three prototype chassis and body designs were being prepared – the V3s. Although later modified after receiving accident damage, V3/1 and V3/2 both initially sported headlamps set on the car's nose. The V3/3, however, took on an altogether more familiar appearance with its smaller headlamps being set directly into the wings. It was also different to the other models in that it featured a smaller rear engine cover, a different windscreen profile and a steel rather than wooden floor pan.

Between 12 October and 22

THE BIRTH OF THE BEETLE

December 1936, each of these three prototypes was driven an astonishing 50,000km across mixed terrain from the wide, smooth concrete expanses of the newly constructed autobahns to the rough, rutted and winding roads of the Black Forest and the punishing climbs of the Alps. The cars survived their ordeal, encountering few problems along the way – except, that is, for an encounter with a deer that resulted in a festive venison feast for the team of test drivers!

Since January 1936, Porsche's bodywork specialist, Erwin Komenda, had been busily working on yet another new design – the V30 (Porsche Type-61K). In an attempt to save significant weight over its predecessors, the car was slightly smaller than before and made use of clever metal-creasing techniques to increase strength while allowing for a lighter, 0.7mm gauge of steel to be used in its construction. A 1:5 scale model was constructed and used for extensive wind tunnel testing – quite an innovation in the 1930s. In preparation for further extensive field tests, Baron von Malberg, financial director of the Porsche company, called established manufacturers Daimler-Benz and

asked for a quote on the production of 30 prototype vehicles. Again, keen to demonstrate his progress, Porsche took an early prototype VW30 to Munich to show off to a delighted Führer.

To assist in the testing of the V30, a team of 60 SS personnel, all sworn to the strictest secrecy, were recruited to act as drivers. Only after recruiting was complete did it transpire that some of the test drivers could not actually drive at all!

The 30 cars were divided into basic testing groups – autobahn, town, country and a mixture of all three – and were driven almost non-stop over the coming months with every single kilometre being painstakingly logged. The culmination of the trial was an extended Alpine run which took the cars high into the mountains and across the border into the north of Italy. The cars were then driven over the infamous Turracher Höhe, the steepest pass in the Eastern Alps with gradients reaching 33%, and the Grossglockner Pass, at 2504m the highest in Austria. Over the course of just a few months the 30 cars had been driven a colossal 1,943,658km with one of the prototypes alone

On the sign: Edelweisspitze 8·1 km, Ferleiten 18·8 km, Zell am See 39·2 km, Salzburg 127·4 km, Franz Josefs Höhe 14·9 km, Heiligenblut 14·4 km, Lienz 53·7 km, Kärntner Seen. HOCHTOR PARKPLATZ 2503 m ü.d. M.

clocking up an astounding 120,478 km.

With the technical side almost complete, another question raised its head: who was to build the new Volkswagen and where?

A decision was made to put the *Kraft durch Freude* (KdF) division of the government-sponsored (and only) national trade union, the *Deutsche Arbeitsfront* or DAF, in charge of production. The thinking of the RDA was that such a cheap car for the working classes should not unduly impact on their own established high-end trade – therefore why not let the workers themselves build the cars? A new company was formed – *Gesellschaft zur Vorbereitung des Deutschen Volkswagens mbH* (Gezuvor for short – a German play on words meaning

ABOVE Testing the V30 on the infamous Grossglockner Pass in Austria

"go ahead") – the Organisation for the Preparation of the German People's Car. Based in Berlin and at the Porsche offices in Stuttgart, it appointed three directors – Hitler's automotive advisor Jakob Werlin of Daimler-Benz, Dr Bodo Lafferentz, a senior DAF official, and Ferdinand Porsche.

Lafferentz chartered a light aircraft to help him find a suitable site for the factory. A location was chosen near the Lower Saxony town of Fallersleben in the north of the country. Its position was ideal, being situated on the banks of the Mittelland Canal (the principal

waterway joining Berlin with the industrial heartland of the Ruhr Valley), the primary east–west autobahn and the main railway link between Hanover and Berlin. The only objection came from the owner of the land, Count von der Schulenburg, whose ancestors had been granted the land as reward for defending the region against Slavic invaders in the 12th century. Eventually the count, unable to use his influence in Berlin, was forced to sell so the stage was set for the construction of the largest motor factory this side of the Atlantic.

Meanwhile, the final modifications were being made to the Volkswagen's design. The most significant of these was the inclusion for the first time of a rear window. The car's rear profile had been carefully designed with aerodynamics in mind but the use of matching curved glass would have been prohibitively expensive. Instead, a split rear oval screen was created using standard flat glass. With sloping lights added at Ferdinand Porsche's request, the final production model was designated, on paper at least, the VW38. Hitler, however was about to drop a bombshell.

On 26 May 1938, a huge ceremony attended by all of the Nazi hierarchy was organised to mark the laying of the first foundation stone. To the horror of Ferdinand Porsche and all of his team, the Führer announced that, in honour of the DAF organisation entrusted with its construction, the new car would be known as the KdF-Wagen and the new town being built to house the workforce would be called KdF-Stadt. Not exactly the most catchy of names for a car – especially where the export market was concerned!

Soon afterwards a purchase plan was announced that would have, in theory, allowed the working man to purchase his very own KdF-Wagen. A savings scheme was devised whereby a worker could save between 5 RM and 15 RM per week towards the cost of the car. After 750 RM had been paid an order number would be issued. There were to be no third party dealers to mark up the price – the whole process was to be administered by the KdF and the DAF. *"Fünf mark die Woche musst Du sparen – willst Du im eignen Wagen fahren!"* – *"Five marks a week you must put aside, if in your own car you want to ride!"*

Approximately 336,000 German citizens signed up for the scheme, many of them saving pfennigs and marks they could ill afford. Circumstances were, however, about to conspire against their dreams of realising car ownership. With the spectre of global conflict on the horizon, the barely complete KdF factory was turned over to war production. As a result, not a single person received a car through the scheme. The KdF-Wagen, meanwhile, was about to don a whole new set of clothes as it prepared to go to war.

LEFT The VW30 – a triumph of engineering

BELOW The production KdF-Wagen

Sporting Ambitions

Throughout his professional career, Ferdinand Porsche had shown a great deal of interest in motor racing and in the quest for speed. His early System Lohner-Porsche design had broken numerous Austrian speed records and the man himself had driven a front-wheel drive Mixte to victory in the prestigious 1901 Exelberg Rally near Vienna. His passion for speed had continued during his time at Austro-Daimler with the creation of the Sascha racing car (named after the eccentric sportsman Count Alexander "Sascha" Kolowrat – a colourful character known for racing with his pet pig strapped into the passenger seat) and at Daimler-Benz in Stuttgart, where he developed the iconic SSK. To crown his racing achievements, in 1932 he was responsible for the development of the magnificent and all-conquering

16-cylinder Auto Union "Silver Arrows" Grand Prix car – a machine which all but dominated the world of motor sport until the outbreak of the Second World War. It was clear that, when it came to sheer speed, Germany was already the world leader on the race track, but Porsche also wanted to extend that prestige to the road.

Initial plans to develop a high-speed road car based on the Volkswagen and with government support were met with short shrift by the DAF; the whole purpose of the Volkswagen project was, after all, to produce a working car for the working man. Undeterred, Porsche and his team set to designing a sports car of their own.

Still based on the Volkswagen concept, the Type 114 Sportwagen (known in-house as the F-Wagen in honour of Ferdinand Porsche

himself) was, in effect, based on a stretched KdF-Wagen powered by an innovatively designed 1.5-litre water-cooled V10 with domed pistons and triple-carburettors for maximum power output – cold starting and fuel economy were not of the highest priority for this project! Once again, Reimspiess was employed to create an advanced and aerodynamic body design. Instructed to keep his plan to the style of the Volkswagen, his aluminium skinned creation with its domed roof and split rear screen was the most stunning of designs. His creation was undeniably Beetle-esque in its styling but sadly, with war on the horizon, the nearest the Sportwagen got to production was a single beautifully sculpted wooden scale model constructed for wind tunnel tests.

ABOVE The great Berndt Rosemeyer at the wheel of the Auto Union Type C in the 1936 German Grand Prix

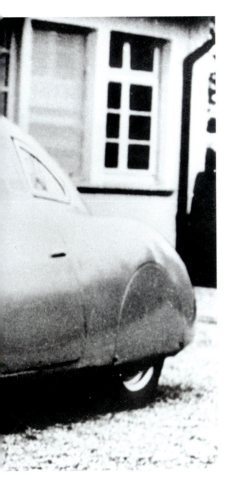

There was, however, one pre-war sporting "Beetle" which did make it on to the road – the incredible Type 64 KdF Rekordwagen.

Early in 1938, Porsche had made an ally of SS Major Adolf Hühnlein, the head of the *Nationalsozialistischen Kraftfahrkorps* (NSKK) – an organisation with the responsibility of promoting motoring interests within the Reich. By a happy coincidence, Hühnlein also happened to be in charge of the *Oberste Nationale Sportbehöde* (ONS), which was responsible for the organisation and administration of all Germany's motor sport activity. Hühnlein also knew people who could make things happen – his personal friend Adolf Hitler being one of them.

Later that year, a new competition was announced to the industry – a gruelling 1,500km road race from Berlin to Rome. Planned to take place in September 1939, it would run on the newly constructed autobahn from Berlin to Munich, then on to Austria and across the Alps to Italy via the Brenner Pass before heading due south to the Italian capital.

Sensing a publicity coup in the

making, three cars were ordered from Porsche by Volkswagen to participate in the race. Similar in many respects to the Type 114, the design created by Karl Fröhlich featured sweeping lines, a domed roof and covered wheels. The passenger seat was offset 30cm to that of the driver's to accommodate an enlarged 50-litre fuel tank, while weight was kept to a minimum by constructing the bodywork out of aluminium and the chassis, pedals and fittings from a special alloy called duralumin. For additional weight saving, baffles were omitted from the silencer!

Although the race, for obvious reasons, was never actually run, all three cars were produced. The first, finished in August 1939, was given to Volkswagenwerk director Dr Bodo Lafferentz who drove the car for just a short time until his enthusiasm overtook his ability and he crashed. The second and third cars, finished in December 1939 and June 1940 respectively, were used extensively by the Porsche family during the war years before being stored out of harm's way in a barn at a gliding school near Zell am See in the Austrian state of Salzburg. Both survived

the war only for car number two to be "requisitioned" by some American troops billeted nearby who proceeded to cut off the roof and run it until the engine seized and it was scrapped.

Fortunately, car number three saw a happier ending. Recovered by Ferdinand Porsche's son, Ferry, it was first registered in Austria before being sent to Italy for bodywork repairs at the workshops of Pininfarina. With its engine reconditioned and the car back to its former glory, a new badge was fashioned for the front of the car; it simply read Porsche – the first car to actually bear the family name. The car was later sold to one-armed Austrian sports car enthusiast Otto Mathé, who at last allowed the Porsche Type 64 to do what it was designed to do – race! Blisteringly fast and surprisingly competitive,

its finest hour was in winning the 1950 Alpine Cup – an achievement which earned Mathé the personal congratulations of Ferdinand Porsche.

Visitors to the new Porsche Museum in Stuttgart are greeted by the sight of a replica Type 64 as they enter. The only remaining original car is thought to reside in a private collection in Austria.

LEFT The only surviving Type 64 on display at a special exhibition in Hamburg

BELOW TA replica Type 64 at the Porsche museum, Stuttgart

The War Years

RIGHT The amphibious Schimmwagen

As far back as 1934 and the publication of Ferdinand Porsche's Exposé, there had been talk of the possible dual military applications of the Volkswagen but it wasn't until 1938 that such discussion became a reality.

At the request of the German high command, a new vehicle was to be developed. It was to be lightweight, inexpensive to build, capable of performing well both on and off road and able to demonstrate reliability in the most extreme conditions. With its waterless, air-cooled motor incapable of freezing in the cold of winter or boiling up in the heat of the desert, the humble Volkswagen seemed an excellent starting point and within a month the first prototype was ready for testing.

It was realised from the very outset that the standard Volkswagen chassis wouldn't be resilient enough to endure the day-in, day-out wear and tear that military use would inflict upon it. Various designs were investigated until, after much toing and froing,

first the Type 62 and then the Type 82 Kübelwagen were produced – the name being derived from *kübelsitzwagen* or bucket-seat-car; a description which amply described the primitive seating arrangement in the car's original prototype form.

Appearing in various guises throughout the war, the Kübelwagen proved to be the most effective of vehicles. More than capable of speeding along metalled roads at a brisk 80 km/h, it would also happily trundle at walking pace for hour after hour without complaint or breakdown, while its lack of four-wheel drive was easily offset by its svelte 550 kg operational weight.

Another Volkswagen military offshoot was the innovative and rather unique Schwimmwagen – a fully amphibious jeep that was capable of 80 km/h on road or a speedy 10 km/h on water thanks to its buoyant water-tight design and triple-blade propeller driven by three chains from a modified crankshaft.

Also produced was the striking and purposeful Kommandeurwagen – effectively a later Type 86 (four-wheel drive) raised Kübelwagen chassis combined with a VW38 Beetle body with widened wings and huge Kronprinz tyres. Impressive and imposing in every respect, it was a great favourite of senior officers of the regular army and the SS.

Aside from military vehicle production, the Volkswagen plant at KdF-Stadt was also used for the production of aircraft fuel tanks, 500 kg bombs, torpedo bodies and 1.5 million lightweight cooking stoves. Wings, tails and engine

parts for the infamous JU88 Stuka dive bombers were also manufactured at the factory as were, from March 1944, 19,000 V1 flying bombs.

Unsurprisingly, towards the latter stages of the war, the site became a regular target for Allied bombing raids and sustained a great deal of damage. But, as time would tell, there was life in the Fallersleben plant yet!

ABOVE A Holzbrenner "wood-burning" Kübelwagen, 1942

From the Rubble

RIGHT Production resumes at Wolfsburg

Peace finally came to KdF-Stadt in the spring of 1945 when, on 10 April, the troops of the American 102nd Infantry Division rolled through en route to Berlin. With general production halted, a small repair facility was set up within the halls of the Volkswagen plant for the repair of Allied military vehicles overseen by a committee made up of former department heads.

In desperate need of reliable military transport, the controlling local US administration ordered that production of the Kübelwagen should be restarted – albeit on a very small scale – utilising a mix and match of components already held in stock at the factory. Although only 133 Kübelwagens were actually produced for the US army, this single order perhaps saved the entire Volkswagen plant and its contents from being cannibalised for other uses and being lost for ever.

Following the Axis surrender on 8 May, the German economy was decentralised with a view to reducing industrial output to pre-war levels. The Potsdam Agreement divided the country into four zones of occupation – American, British, French and Soviet. With agreements in place permitting the occupying nations to extract war reparations, a great deal of the industrial might housed within the Soviet zone was simply dismantled and shipped back to Mother Russia. Lower Saxony, and with it KdF-Stadt and the Volkswagen factory, thankfully fell under the control of the British.

With the British occupation came a man who was to become the saviour of the Volkswagen Beetle; Major Ivan Hirst of the Royal Electrical and Mechanical Engineers (REME). An experienced engineer, Hirst arrived at KdF-Stadt in early August having previously been in charge of the construction of a central tank repair shop in Brussels, where he had gained valuable practical experience in managing local workforces and dealing with the inevitable material shortages.

The KdF-Stadt that greeted the young officer was one of desolation. The town itself was far from the working utopia envisaged by its Nazi creators. Only the modern layout of its unusually wide open boulevards hinted at the glory that had once been imagined. Instead, Hirst found a maze of rudimentary wooden huts and shacks. The town had originally been planned to accommodate 100,000 but even with its influx of refugees and displaced persons it only housed 25,000 inhabitants. Those present, however,

were of a staggering assortment of nationalities – Poles, Hungarians, French, Danes and Russians were all represented, as were a surprising mix of Brazilians, South Africans, Mexicans, Cubans and Iranians. At this time there were some 21 million refugees moving about Europe looking for somewhere to call home.

Like the Americans before them, the Royal Electrical & Mechanical Engineers initially set up a repair workshop in the Volkswagen works. At this point, the dismantling of the factory and the removal of its machinery seemed all but inevitable. Hirst immediately arranged to meet with Rudolf Brörmann, a former head of quality control who had been installed as factory manager by the Americans. Unlike many other senior managers who had feared for their own safety and wellbeing, Brörmann had not fled the factory at the first signs of arrival of the Allied troops; instead he had consolidated efforts to ensure the survival of the factory. Familiar with the plant, its operations and with the town, Brörmann was to prove a valuable asset to Hirst.

Incredibly, despite the Allied forces' best efforts to disable the factory by dropping over 2,000 bombs on it, the Volkswagen plant was in surprisingly good condition with only 30% of the factory buildings and a mere 8% of the machinery having been destroyed. Kübelwagen production was, therefore, allowed to continue in very small numbers; however, one of Hirst's superiors was more than aware of the factory's true potential.

Based at REME headquarters in Bad Oeynhausen, Colonel Michael A. McEvoy had spent time before the war living in the city of Stuttgart, where he had worked for Mercedes-Benz on the development of the Silver Arrows racing cars. In 1939, he had seen the KdF-Wagen at the Berlin Motor Show and remembered it with great fondness. What better solution to help service the British Army's desperate need for light transportation? he reasoned. McEvoy soon found an ally in Hirst and the pair hatched a plan to bring the car to the attention of the military bigwigs. The most pristine remaining Volkswagen was made spick and span and given a business-like coat of khaki paint before being driven to headquarters for inspection. The car, seen as an ideal short-term solution, was greeted with general approval and an order was placed on 22 August 1945 for an astounding 20,000 saloons, 500 vans and 700 trailers.

With the Volkswagen plant offered a new lease of life, the same was offered to KdF-Stadt which, as part of the ongoing denazification process being implemented across the nation, was renamed Wolfsburg after the nearby 14th

BELOW One of the first post-war Volkswagens built for the British military

century Wolfsburg Castle.

Work was undertaken to clear the vast halls of the Wolfsburg plant of bomb damage and debris and the canvas sheeting that covered the enormous metal presses was removed. Tools, dies and other machinery that had been removed and stored away from the main plant were reinstalled. Resuming production was a slow and difficult process but the resilient workforce persevered until the first 55 cars rolled off the "assembly line" that December. Sourcing raw materials proved to be the hardest task and because of this production was a drawn out process. However, in March 1946 there was cause for celebration as the factory and its workers commemorated their first month in which 1,000 cars had been produced – a rate at which production was able to continue for some months. By the end of 1946, 10,020 cars had been manufactured.

With the factory now beginning to look like a viable concern, permission was granted to offer the Volkswagen plant a four-year stay of execution over which time it could not be dismantled or stripped of its assets as war reparation. Soon after, agreement was reached to establish a sales network for Volkswagen cars within the British sector, consisting of two main distributors and 28 local dealerships.

It was, however, all very well this German factory earning German money from German customers but there was a greater issue still needing to be addressed; an issue which had an impact on an international scale. Britain and more specifically the British taxpayers, who were themselves still subject to shortages and rationing, were bearing the lion's share of the cost of importing food and essentials into Germany's British Zone. To compound matters, payments had to be made in US dollars. For German industry to recover, it would need to earn foreign currency of its own, and the only way to do that was to export.

Displayed at the Hanover Export Fair in August 1947, the Volkswagen gained its first authorised international sales through *Pon's Automobielhandel* after Dutch importer Ben Pon and his brother took five cars to Holland. By the turn of the year, this number had increased to 56. Contracts were then signed with importers in Switzerland, Belgium, Luxembourg, Sweden, Denmark and Norway and within a year the volume of exported Volkswagens had increased to 4,385 – about 15% of the total manufactured.

LEFT Bombed but not out of business

The Export Model

RIGHT A 1950
Export model
Beetle

As business steadily grew for the fledgling company, 1948 saw a number of key changes take place at the top of the Volkswagen tree. The most significant of these was the appointment of Heinz Nordhoff to the position of chief trustee and director general replacing accountant Dr Hermann Münch, whose lack of technical expertise was beginning to impact negatively on the business.

Nordhoff brought with him a wealth of valuable experience, having managed the Opel plant in Brandenburg during the war. He was dismissed from the factory by the American Military administration and had since found work in Hamburg as a customer service manager, where his obvious abilities had instantly caught the eye of Ivan Hirst. On his employment, Nordhoff was instructed to work closely with Hirst and to involve him whenever he was required. But Nordhoff was not only an engineer through and through but a skilled and dedicated manager, and soon

Hirst realised that his days of usefulness at the plant were numbered.

Hirst left Volkswagen in the spring of 1949 having truly brought the company back from the brink of extinction. On his departure he was presented with a beautifully crafted scale model of a Beetle – a possession he treasured until his death in 2000.

1949 was also significant in that it was the year that the Wolfsburg plant and Volkswagen itself were finally relinquished by the British Military Government and handed over to the State of Lower Saxony. Once again Volkswagen was a truly German company.

Nordhoff's influence on the company was both instant and long standing. It was he who introduced a guiding principle of constant refinement and improvement rather than constant replacement – a policy very much at odds with the way the automobile market was developing in the resource-rich United States, where the annual release of new models was seen as a way

of driving sales. What upwardly mobile salesman would want to be seen in a '49 Coupe de Ville when his neighbour was driving round in a 1950 model? Nordhoff knew he had a sound product; his challenge was to ensure it capitalised on all possible markets.

The Beetle had, of course, been built to a purposeful but basic no–frills specification. It was undoubtedly a superb piece of design both mechanically and aesthetically but, in the eyes of the international markets that Nordhoff sought to conquer, to describe the Volkswagen as spartan might be seen as over glamorisation.

The answer was the introduction of the "Export" model (known as the Deluxe in its native Germany). With an all-round higher specification and improved build quality, it was specifically designed to capture the imagination of the world's importing nations.

Initially the Export models sported few mechanical improvements; instead the changes were of a more cosmetic nature. The flat painted bumpers were replaced with smooth, reshaped chrome plated ones complete with stylish over-riders. Chrome was also used for the

THE EXPORT MODEL

RIGHT A later Export model still retaining its characteristic split oval rear screen

hubcaps, door handles and headlamp surrounds (although these items remained unpainted on the still available standard models destined for the domestic German market). The bonnet featured smart aluminium trim, the front wings with small grilles (one to increase audibility of the now concealed horn, the other purely to maintain symmetry). The boot now proudly sported a gleaming silver VW insignia.

Internally there was no shortage of enhanced trim or brightwork. The previously black knobs and buttons were now finished in ivory with a sporty two-spoke steering wheel to match. The seats were now fully adjustable (even for rake) and the carpets were selected to match the colour of the cars' paintwork, which now extended past dull greys and blacks to pastel greens, Bordeaux reds, medium browns and pearl greys. Like a cinematic production, the Volkswagen Beetle was moving from being a black and white silent movie to a full-blown Technicolor performance with concert sound.

Significant mechanical improvements started to appear in 1950, when VW's now outdated cable brakes were replaced by more modern hydraulic alternatives.

Internal ventilation was also improved, although there is still ongoing debate about the true effectiveness of the vent flaps that were fitted to the car's front quarter panels – known affectionately as "crotch-coolers". It is fair to say that their over-zealous breezy properties are not to every driver's or passenger's taste, especially if a short skirt or lightweight trousers are being worn.

The following year, further changes included the fitment of double action telescopic shock absorbers to replace the

inadequate and outmoded single lever units and the addition of chrome trim to the windscreen surround. A further addition was an exquisite full-coloured enamel bonnet badge featuring the Wolfsburg crest – a modified version of the Schulenburg coat-of-arms paying tribute to the grand estate upon which the Volkswagen plant had originally been constructed.

More significant modifications were made in late 1952. Stronger, more modern bumpers with large over-riders were fitted, adding both to the car's looks and to its safety, whilst wider tyres running at a lower pressure softened the ride and did wonders for passenger comfort. All of the windows and not just the windscreen were now treated to a highly polished brightwork surround. Internally, the updated design was even more apparent with a completely redesigned dashboard with the new speedometer now located directly above the steering wheel and large central grille to accommodate a radio speaker if fitted. Produced only between October 1952 and March 1953, these somewhat rare examples are commonly known by Volkswagen devotees as Oval Dash Splits or *"Zwitters"*.

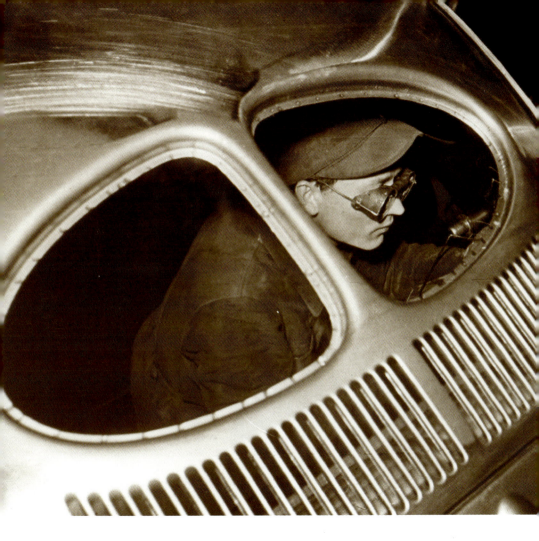

The Hebmüller Coupé

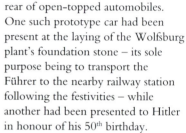

From the very outset, Ferdinand Porsche had envisaged the production of a convertible Volkswagen to complement the standard production model – indeed it should be remembered that the project's original godfather had something of a penchant for standing up in the rear of open-topped automobiles. One such prototype car had been present at the laying of the Wolfsburg plant's foundation stone – its sole purpose being to transport the Führer to the nearby railway station following the festivities – while another had been presented to Hitler in honour of his 50th birthday.

In 1949, the time finally arrived to consider the manufacture of a Beetle cabriolet; however, with even the most basic of material resources still scarce on the ground and the Wolfsburg plant already running close to capacity, Nordhoff was quick to realise that its design and production would have to take place elsewhere. There was no shortage of competent and creative coachbuilders ready and willing to take on the task but two firms soon came to the fore – Wilhelm Karmann of Osnabrück and Hebmüller and Sons of Wuppertal – both of whom had already been in business for over 60 years. Karmann was duly awarded a contract

to produce a four-seat cabriolet while Hebmüller was licensed to create a two-seat coupé.

Based on the 1945/46 Volkswagen saloon, the first Hebmüller prototypes suffered from excessive chassis flex, resulting in continuously misaligned panels and cracks in the windscreen glass. After several rounds of modification in which the sills were strengthened and reinforcing bars were mounted across the width of the chassis, these problems were, however, solved.

Available in black, white or red (with two-tone options also being rather popular), the final design of the Hebmüller coupé was very striking. Rather than rework or modify existing panels and fitments, many had been created from scratch – the most gorgeous examples of this being the stunningly crafted engine cover, the characteristic single brake light mounted just above the rear number plate and the superbly engineered (and highly expensive) waterproof roof that folded away to become completely unseen within the car's bodywork.

Although costly in comparison to its standard saloon brother, the Hebmüller proved to be a great success. It was, however, destined to enjoy but a short time in production. In July 1949, a fire started in the paint shop and swept its

way through the Hebmüller factory. Production eventually restarted but, by then, the damage had already been done – Hebmüller was financially crippled and the company finally went bankrupt in 1952.

During its brief life, a mere 750 Hebmüller coupés were manufactured, making it one of the most desirable Volkswagen Beetles ever produced.

The Oval Arrives

For any Beetle enthusiast, one of the truly defining moments in the Bug's history took place in March 1953 when the VW's split rear screen was lost forever; replaced by a single gently curving sheet of oval-shaped safety glass. Offering a significant 23% increase in area, it not only improved rear visibility but also softened the over all appearance of the car – a gentler look for a gentler time. The Oval was born.

The Oval's numerous significant changes were, however, not solely confined to its cosmetic refinements. Gone, at last, was the old 1192cc 25PS (24.7bhp) engine of wartime origin – in its place sat a new and more powerful 1131cc 30PS (29.6bhp) motor with an enlarged bore, widened inlet valves and an increased compression ratio. The resulting improvement in power and performance offered a top speed of 66.1 mph and a 0-60 mph of 34 seconds – almost laughable figures in modern times but a] leap forward for the Beetle back in the early 1950s.

Across the Atlantic, sales of the Beetle had been torturously slow to pick up. Dutch exporter Ben Pon, the mastermind behind the VW Transporter, had first tried to introduce the Volkswagen to North America in 1949 when he took a single car to the United States in an attempt to convince dealers. America, however, was entering an age where bigger was always seen as better. Branded "Hitler's Car" and "the Victory Wagon", the little Wagen from Wolfsburg failed to impress.

Pon's efforts were soon followed by those of Austrian born Max Hoffman: an ex-racing driver who had turned his hand to importing European cars to sell through his landmark Frank Lloyd Wright-designed showroom in New York's exclusive Park Avenue. It was he who would first introduce MG, Jaguar, Healey, Porsche, and later Mercedes-Benz, BMW and Alfa Romeo to the American public. However, selling the Beetle to a market that was yet to appreciate its unique charm

proved to be hard going – even for Hoffman. In 1953, after four years of hard work with little reward, Hoffman gladly relinquished his distributorship contract with VW – a decision which, later in life, the affluent automotive entrepreneur admitted to be his greatest ever misjudgement.

Still convinced that the stateside market was there for the taking, Heinz Nordhoff made the decision that, rather than appointing any more third-party distributors, Volkswagen itself should establish a North American sales and distribution organisation of its own. For ease of purpose, the country arbitrarily divided into two territories; Will Van de Kamp was appointed to look after the company's interests in the east and Geoffrey Lange the west. Despite being very different characters with their own unique ways of working, the pair had, within a year of starting, achieved far more than their predecessors had ever thought possible.

In 1949, Pon's efforts had resulted in just two cars being sold in the United States – the very two he, himself, had taken as sales samples. Hoffman started his period as distributor selling 157 cars in 1950. Sales picked up over the years but he was never to come close to his bold declaration that he would soon be selling 3,000 Bugs every month; his best monthly effort during his four year tenure being a rather modest 160 cars with his peak annual sale in 1953 being just over 1,000 Volkswagens.

In 1955, the combined efforts of Van de Kamp and Lange saw this annual figure leap over six-fold to 6,614 units. A year later this jumped dramatically

RIGHT The one-millionth Beetle

once again, with almost 31,000 cars reaching the American market. Combined with exported European, South American and Australian sales, Volkswagen was now selling over 55% of its production outside of Germany.

With sales in the States on the increase, it became necessary to develop models with alternative specifications to those sold in Europe in order to comply with the numerous rules and regulations which governed car design and safety in North America. Beetles destined for America and Canada were the first to be fitted with sealed beam headlamps and, more significantly, wing-mounted indicators instead of the traditional but thoroughly outdated semaphores which featured on European models. Once changed, essential at the time but still popular with Volkswagen enthusiasts to this day, was the fitting of modified front and rear bumpers featuring outsized over-riders with additional tubular bars mounted above the standard bladed fender. Although these are often seen as a highly attractive addition to the Beetle's looks, their inclusion was not a cosmetic consideration. American drivers were not used to the low ride height of the little German car and, quite simply, found parking manoeuvres all but impossible to conduct without causing untold numbers of scrapes and scuffs. In May 1955, another popular design amendment was introduced when American model vehicles were fitted with twin chromed exhausts instead of the single plain steel one offered previously.

Later that same year, on 5 August, Volkswagen reached a landmark in production when the millionth Beetle manufactured since the war rolled off the assembly line.

In celebration, this bodywork of this car was given a luscious coat of glistering gold paint while its bumpers and trim were bedecked with shimmering jewels.

The Karmann
Cabriolet

Whereas the production life of the stunning Hebmüller coupé was sadly cut short following the factory fire of 1949, its four-seat sister car – the Karmann Cabriolet – was set to enjoy a long and prosperous life as one of

Volkswagen's most desirable models.

Like the Hebmüller, early prototypes were based on the 1945/46 model saloons and, with the roof removed, suffered from similar body-flexing problems; an issue resolved by the addition of weighty steel rails welded into the bottom plate of each sill. To iron out this and any other

problems, a total of 25 pre-production Karmanns were rigorously tested before manufacturing commenced in 1949. An initial order for 2,000 cars in August of that year was doubled just eight months later. An instant success, almost 2,700 Karmanns were sold in 1950, rising to 3,958 in 1951. By the end of the decade, Karmann Cabriolet sales were approaching 11,000 cars.

As could be expected from a specialist coachbuilder such as Karmann, the Cabriolet's signature was its outstanding engineering and build quality; the superbly designed folding roof being a perfect case in point. Stretched over a hand-crafted varnished wood and metal frame, it was constructed using layers of rubber and horsehair covered with vinyl or, in some cases, luxurious mohair. Unusual for such a car, especially one aimed at the budget end of the market, its rear-view window was glass rather than clear plastic which was notoriously

vulnerable to creasing and cracking with age. However, unlike the Hebmüller, the Karmann Cabriolet's hood didn't fold away completely into the body; instead it stood proud and high perched above the engine cover. Whilst this did little to detract from the Bug's curiously aesthetic charm it did somewhat detract from the driver's ability to see what was going on behind. Only in 1972, 23 years after the first Cabriolet rolled out of Karmann's Osnabrück plant, was the roof redesigned sufficiently to allow it to fold down 5cm lower. Fortunately, few customers were put off by this minor discrepancy.

CONVERTIBLE

Years of Change

RIGHT A true car of the people, by the 1960s the Beetle was a common sight on Europe's roads

The Beetle underwent further significant change in 1958. Up front the car's A-pillars were slimmed down, allowing the windscreen to be enlarged by 17%. However, more obvious to the casual observer were the changes at the rear; the traditional oval screen having been dropped in favour of an all-new near rectangular replacement. Being an incredible 95% larger in area, this not only made sitting in the rear of the car a less claustrophobic affair but also, more significantly, offered an enormous improvement in visibility. Internally the dashboard was given a complete design overhaul the basic layout of which would stay with the Beetle for the rest of its production life. Finally, the outdated and outmoded roller accelerator that had been a feature since the 1930s was replaced with a thoroughly modern and altogether more responsive conventional treadle type.

To meet type approval and unique to the North American market, the bullet indicators were replaced with teardrop

shaped ones mounted cleanly on the apex of the front wings.

For all of its continuous development and design merit, one handling characteristic that had plagued the Beetle from its very inception was the

car's tendency to dramatically oversteer under certain driving conditions, caused by a combination of narrow track, swing axle suspension and uneven weight distribution thanks to the rear-mounted engine. The handling of the 1960 model

Beetle took a quantum leap forward thanks to the welcome addition of a simple front anti-roll bar and the lowering of the pivot point of the rear swing axle. Compared to traditional front-engined automobiles, the Bug was still obviously tail heavy but the modifications provided drivers with a noticeable improvement in handling and road holding.

The Beetle driving experience was further enhanced a year later with the long overdue inclusion of a full synchromesh transmission and a new 34 PS engine of a type already fitted to the ubiquitous VW Transporter. Designed

RIGHT A 1965
Beetle 1300

with a strengthened crankcase, improved crankshaft and a wider spacing of the cylinder barrels, it utilised a smaller crankshaft pulley and large dynamo pulley – the combination resulting in significantly less engine noise thanks to the slower running cooling fan and a good increase in useable power. Top speed was now up to about 72 mph while acceleration from 0-50 mph was now achievable in less than 18 seconds. A flatter profiled redesign of the petrol tank released a good deal more space in the front luggage compartment (an increase from 85 litres to a more accommodating 140 litres) and, at long, long last, European customers joined those in the States in being treated to the modern delights of flashing filament indicators in place of the old, unpopular and incredibly outmoded semaphore signals.

After years of rattling along in the dark ages, more "modern" additions were made to the Beetle in 1962; all VWs, not just the upmarket export model, were fitted with hydraulic rather than mechanical brakes while, inside, the dash was now adorned with yet another luxury in the form of a fuel gauge. Until that time you just had to wait for the engine to cough and splutter before switching a tap to release an emergency get-you-home gallon of fuel into the system.

Although there were very few major changes to the Beetle over the next couple of years, the Volkswagen company itself continued to expand at a phenomenal rate. Driven by a change in import regulations, VW stopped shipping cars to Mexico; instead choosing to establish Volkswagen de México SA de CV and a factory in Mexico City. Such was the humble Bug's meteoric rise to stardom in the country, a second plant was constructed just a year later in the city of Puebla.

By this time, back home in Germany an impressive 33% of the domestic car market and 50% of the light commercial market was dominated by VW and, as a whole, Volkswagen was producing twice as many cars as any of its European-based rivals. In order to cope with demand, another huge facility was constructed. Located on the north coast of the country just a few miles from the Dutch border and dealing exclusively with the manufacture of export models, the Emden plant included its own

privately owned seaport.

1964 heralded the arrival of the VW1300 with further enlarged windows, flat hubcaps replacing the stylish domed ones that had graced the Beetle throughout its entire post-war life and a more powerful 1285cc 40bhp. To the casual observer, the only distinguishing mark to set it aside from other VW models was a silver "1300" badge positioned jauntily on the engine lid. Although noticeably quicker than its predecessors and enjoying performance to match all of its contemporary European rivals the 1300 was, however, a short-lived addition to the range.

The '67 Special

Launched in late 1966 for the '67 model year, the VW1500 is regarded by many enthusiasts as the most desirable of all Beetles combining, as it does, the very best elements of the classic design with the infinitely more driveable nature of its improved engine and enhanced handling characteristics.

The heart of the VW1500 was its 1493cc engine. With an enlarged bore and increased compression ratio, it produced a creditable 44bhp at 4,000 rpm but reached its maximum torque low down in the rev-range at just 2,800 rpm to offer a higher top speed and better acceleration with little or no penalty on fuel consumption. An increased rear track, now some 100mm wider than Porsche's original, improved cornering stability. Although hidden under the now standard flat hubcaps, four bolts retained the wheels rather than the five from before. Stopping power was also increased thanks to the fitting of front disk brakes. Curiously, however, this seemingly obvious

benefit to driver and passenger safety was to remain absent from all North America-bound Beetles throughout its entire production life. Safety was also in mind when it came to the interior styling. All chrome trim and other reflective surfaces were removed with all the buttons and switches now being manufactured in black and from softer, more impact-resistant materials.

Externally, the engine lid was subtly remodelled to bring the number plate positioning in line with stringent US regulations while, up front, the Beetle took on a slightly different look thanks to new sealed-beam headlights set vertically against reshaped wings.

The welcome arrival of the VW1500 did, however, coincide with a sad departure from Volkswagen's automotive empire. Having already announced his retirement from the position he had held for 20 years, Heinz Nordhoff died suddenly on 12 April 1968. During his time with the company he had witnessed annual production of the Beetle rise

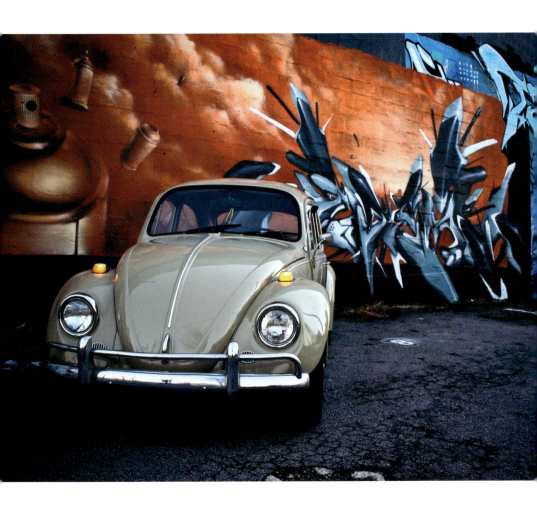

from 19,244 cars in 1948 to a staggering 1,186,134 during his final year in office. Ferdinand Porsche may well have fathered the Beetle and Ivan Hurst was undoubtedly responsible for resurrecting it from the ashes but, where so many other manufacturers had constantly sought to replace perfectly good existing models, it was Nordhoff's desire and obsession with the perfection of this single car that had made the Volkswagen Beetle a truly global and unparalleled success story.

Die Neuen Käfer

Da weiß man, was man hat.

Many consider 1968 to be a year in which the Beetle underwent a significant revamp; a quick glance at VW promotional material of the time in which the company heralded the arrival of "*Die Neuen Käfer*" – the New Beetle – could easily convince you that this was the case. The reality, however, was somewhat different.

By this time, VW's policy of being a single model marque was long a thing of the past. Since the introduction of the commercially orientated Transporter in 1950, the Wolfsburg manufacture had given us the sporty Karmann Ghia in 1955 and the curious Type 3 in 1961. In 1968 came the introduction of the best forgotten 411 – an oversized, overpriced and underpowered rust-bucket of a car known with little affection in its native country as the *Nasenbär* (a Brazilian aardvark with a particularly long and ugly nose) or by the term "*Vier Türen elf Jahre zu spät*" – four doors 11 years too late! Executives at Volkswagen were not, therefore, overly disposed to the idea of

investing enormous amounts of money towards the ongoing development of a car which, by this time, was rapidly approaching its 30th birthday; instead, the company continued to offer ever more obscure limited and special edition models in an attempt to maintain

interest in the ageing design. Thankfully, a level of celebrity patronage and its cool swinging sixties appeal had kept the humble VW Bug well in the public eye.

Although perhaps not warranting the grand title of "New Beetle" which had been bestowed upon it by the VW

LEFT "Because you know what you have" proclaims the advertisement

marketing department, the '68 model was in several ways, different from its predecessors. Externally, the upright headlamps that already featured on models destined for the US market were now seen across the entire range and with them a redesigned front wing.

Unfortunately for Beetle owners, this cosmetic modification came with a design fault as the resulting well just below the headlight served as a receptacle for rain water and road salt – a perfect recipe for rust; revised squared bumpers set higher on the body replaced the attractive rounded ones, while the repositioned non-locking fuel filler cap was at last accessed via a simple hinged flap, removing the need to open the entire front bonnet lid each time refuelling was required. Mechanically the most significant change was the fitting of dual circuit brakes – another long overdue safety addition.

With the stick shift-averse US market in mind, an automatic was also introduced into the range – first as an option on the 1500 and then for the 1300. It was, however, not an automatic as we would understand the term today – although the need for depressing a clutch pedal was removed, the gears of the three-speed transmission were still changed manually using a shift lever. The system worked well but at a cost, with fuel consumption reduced to a paltry 25mpg and acceleration to 60 taking the best part of 28 seconds.

Two "luxury" models were also added to the Beetle portfolio in the form of the 1300L and 1500L. Whilst not available in all markets, those that treated themselves to a Bug with an "L" postfix were lavished with a plethora of decadent add-ons including rubber

inserts on the bumpers, reversing lights housed within the rear light clusters, a padded dashboard, a vanity mirror and a pocket in not only the driver's door but the passenger door too.

The Super Beetle

Real change came to the Beetle in the summer of 1971 with the arrival of the VW1302S or Super Beetle. A direct replacement for the previously top-of-the-range 1500, this technically advanced model enjoyed the benefits of MacPherson strut suspension to the front, semi-trailing arms to the rear, double-jointed axles and a substantial anti-roll bar. This modern reworking of the suspension components brought with it the additional benefit of freeing up more space to the front of the car, enabling boot space to be increased by an impressive 85%.

A reshaped body featured rounder wings, a broader and more bulbous bonnet, a longer front bumper and an extended valance. From the side the 1302S was easily identifiable thanks to its crescent-shaped air vents located just behind the rear side windows. To the rear, the engine cover was modified to accommodate the extra height of a new 1600cc engine which, along with its existing 1300cc counterpart, was fitted with a revised twin-port cylinder head for easier breathing – the 1300 now providing 44PS (a credible 10% increase) and the 1600 turning out a healthy 50PS.

Thursday 17 February 1972 was to be an important date in the Volkswagen's

THE SUPER BEETLE

RIGHT The Beetle
overtakes the
Ford Model T
as the world's
most popular
car of all time

long and esteemed history, for it was on this day that the 15,007,034th Beetle rolled off of the Wolfsburg assembly line to finally overtake the iconic Model T Ford as the world's most popular car of all time. In celebration, the special edition 1302S based *"Weltmeister"* was produced for the German market while a more humble torsion-bar 1200 based "World Champion" was created for the United Kingdom. Both models were easily identifiable thanks to their unique marathon blue paintwork and 10-spoke silver-painted steel wheels. Approximately 6,000 of the *Weltmeister* and 1,500 of the World Champion were sold.

The 1302 was, itself, superseded in 1973 with the arrival of the imaginatively named 1303, the most striking feature of which was its bulging over-curved windscreen. Doing little to add to the Beetle's flagging aesthetics, this unattractive innovation grew solely from an intention to satisfy a pending item of US vehicle safety legislation that sought to dramatically increase the distance between seats and windscreen. The regulations never came into effect but the costly modification remained; if nothing else, visibility was at least

ABOVE 1938
to 1976 – the
development of
the Wolfsburg
Beetle

slightly improved.

    With the ageing Beetle now subjected
to a non-existent development budget,
few positive changes were seen to its
specification or design after the summer

of 1973 as Volkswagen now had a new,
exciting and thoroughly modern toy
to shout about. On the drawing board
since 1969 and finally launched in the
spring of 1974, the VW Golf (known

way back in the 1930s. Gone was the air-cooled, rear-mounted and rear-wheel drive layout that had battled on for almost 40 years.In its place was a water-cooled, front-engined, front-wheel drive automotive masterpiece.

With the arrival of the Golf, the writing was clearly on the wall for the Volkswagen Beetle. 1975 saw all but the 1200 models struck from the range. While the basic 1200 was subjected to an ever more basic specification, in a last-gasp attempt to muster further sales, the "top-end" 1200L was made more luxurious than ever.

European production of the VW Beetle finally came to a halt on 19 January 1978 when the 15,444,858[th] German built car rolled off the assembly line at Emden but this was not before a suitable tribute had been paid; resplendent in Diamond Silver paintwork, 300 "Final Edition" Beetles were shipped to the United Kingdom in September 1977. Confusingly, 300 Beetles in other colours were also imported and marketed as "Final Editions". These, however, didn't benefit from the special numbered commemorative plaque that was supplied (in most cases) with the official models.

curiously as the Rabbit in North America) was as far removed from the Beetle in design and technology as Ferdinand Porsche's original People's Car had been from its contemporaries

LITTLE BOOK OF **BEETLE**

Viva Los Vochos!

BELOW The Última Edición - the final Beetle

When European assembly of the Beetle finally came to a halt in January 1978, few could have imagined that the car would still remain in production for another quarter of a century.

Almost immediately, cars built at the Mexican Pueblo plant started to arrive in Europe. For some time, vehicles from this production line had benefited from little more than a spartan specification but, like their North American and European counterparts, the Mexican car-buying public was now insisting on all-round higher standards. The first cars to make the trans-Atlantic voyage were ostensibly the same as the last 1200L cars to leave Emden. There were, however, a handful of differences: the rear window, for example, was of an older style and therefore smaller than its European contemporary. Body trim was bright anodised rather than black painted – as were the protruding tailpipes. More significantly, the tyres were all of a radial construction rather than ageing cross-plies. Few other changes were made until the end of 1981, at which point the engine cover's slotted louvres were lost.

Determined to move on both technologically and from a design

standpoint, the final official shipment of Mexican-built Beetles was delivered in August 1985. This, however, didn't impact on the Bug's popularity with a certain breed of enthusiasts, resulting in a wave of "grey" imports being made available through a network of unofficial independent dealers.

Over the years, as the Mexican Beetle underwent further development, rifling from the inexhaustible VW parts bin became more apparent – each addition adding further to the much needed process of modernisation. Window winders and door locks from the Golf were an early addition, as was the use of a steering wheel taken directly from the increasingly popular Polo – a

part which, itself, was superseded by a Golf replacement in 1988. Customers purchasing imports were, however, often surprised to find the lack of fresh-air window blowers and a heater – items normally considered far from essential in a blistering climate such as to be found in Mexico's provinces.

Under the hood, a refined 1600cc engine took pride of place. An environmentally-friendly two-way catalytic converter was added in 1990 followed by a three-way system just two years later. 1992 also saw the introduction of a deluxe model – badged as a GL in line with Volkswagen's new international model designation – with fuel injection and modified cylinder heads. Chromed hubcaps made a welcome return while inside the cabin the driver was treated to a sporty steering wheel taken straight out of the class-defining Golf GTi. Front disc brakes were added to the package the following year.

A more obvious attempt at modernisation became apparent in 1995. With the deluxe model rebranded as the "Classico" and the standard now known as the "City", in vogue colour-coding

was extended to the headlamp trim and bumpers while the door mirrors, handles, bonnet and boot catches and the window surrounds were finished in starkly contrasting black. This level of trim and specification effectively stayed with the Beetle until 2003, when the final chapter of Ferdinand Porsche's masterpiece drew to a sad close. Thankfully, Volkswagen was determined to commemorate the retirement of its greatest ever achievement in suitable style with its best Beetle ever – the *Última Edición*.

Produced in a limited run of just 3,000 vehicles, it paid tribute by combining the very latest technology and styling with the car's best and most popular retro features. Two suitably classic colour choices were made available – Aquarius Blue and Harvest Moon Beige – both of which were supplemented with an abundance of anodised aluminium and brightwork including a waist strip, bonnet trim and running boards, fully chromed hubcaps on colour-matched painted wheels fitted with white-wall tyres, chrome engine cover and boot-lid catches and chrome door handles. The pièce de résistance was a wonderful modern reworking of the

original Wolfsburg crest – a fitting tribute indeed to the world's most popular car.

The very last car to leave the Pueblo production line – an example in Aquarius Blue – was immediately shipped to the Volkswagen museum, where it stands in tribute to the Beetle's remarkable 58 years of continuous production.

The New Beetle

RIGHT Concept 1 Beetle

With European manufacture long consigned to the history books and Mexican production facing the inevitability of being wound down at some point in the near future, prospects for the continued existence of the Beetle marque appeared to be bleak in the 1990s. But the story of the Beetle has always been one of survival and surprises; never more so than the unexpected reception bestowed on a cheeky little concept car displayed on the Volkswagen stand at the 1994 North American International Auto Show in Detroit.

At this time, Volkswagen was undergoing intense competition in the global market from a plethora of cheap, efficient but, on the whole, uninspiring Japanese imports. Its boxy range – the Polo, Golf, Jetta and Passat – although well built and ergonomically designed were hardly ready to set the world alight. Even the category-killing GTi was facing ever more pressure from an increasing batch of wannabe

pretenders. The German manufacturer did, however, have a trump card to play in the form of two inspired designers, both of whom were graduates from the esteemed Art Centre College of Design in Pasadena, California. Having previously been employed by Audi and Porsche respectively, J Mays and Freeman Thomas returned to California in 1991 to set up VW's all-new American Design Center in Simi Valley. Both were of the opinion that a lighter approach to design was needed – something which would fire up the emotions and would, above all, stand out from the bland automotive crowd.

Their resulting creation – known simply as Concept 1 – was supposed to be nothing more than a styling exercise, but it proved to be a show stealer. Unveiled for the first time at the Detroit show it completely stole the limelight from the efforts of every other manufacturer and one question echoed out through the halls of the exhibition: "When will this new Beetle be on sale?"

Mays and Thomas had understood a
principle that had long been forgotten
in the grey faceless boardrooms of the
motor industry – just as style is nothing
without substance, substance itself is

worth very little without the injection
of a little style.

The pair wowed the market yet again
just a year later when, at the prestigious
Geneva Motor Show, they once again

LITTLE BOOK OF **BEETLE**

RIGHT The New
Beetle is born

exhibited Concept 1. But this time it
had an equally stunning stablemate in
the form of a bright red Concept 1
Cabriolet. Yet more interest was shown
by the public and the media but still
Volkswagen remained non-committal
as to its production. Finally, beaten
down by the pressure of public demand,
Volkswagen relented and, in an unusual
but somewhat inspired move, set up a
free telephone service in the United
States to allow potential customers to
pass on their comments on the design
and on what they wanted out of a car.

Despite its clearly retro styling,
Concept 1 was designed as a thoroughly
modern vehicle. Planned from its
inception as a front-wheel drive,
various power-plants were considered
including petrol, diesel and hybrid
configurations. Early in the realisation
process there were thoughts of using
the existing floor pan of Volkswagen's
successful Polo, but this offered little
in terms of state-of-the-art design and
technology. Instead it was decided to
employ an all-new platform (the PQ34)
created for the market-leading Golf – a
decision which offered the designers
not only more space to play with but

an already planned series of efficient and powerful drivetrain options, from an economic two-litre EFI through to a beefy six-cylinder VR6. Front MacPherson strut suspension was complemented at the rear by that old VW favourite – the torsion bar – while ride quality was improved by the use of big 16-inch wheels which also added to the car's visual appeal and air of quality. An impression of separate fenders and pseudo running boards hinted at times past, as did the original bug styled headlamps. Small front air vents skilfully mimicked the horn grilles of the early cars while the big read-lighting pops echoed those of the last Super Beetles.

Inside the car, the driver was presented with an oversized speedometer while the dashboard, although very deep to accommodate the highly raked, sweeping front screen, was inset with painted panels matching the car's exterior bodywork. Essential, state-of-the-art modern safety features such as air bags, side impact bars and multiple crumple zones contrasted perfectly with the whimsical addition of a cheeky little bud vase attached to the dashboard.

Manufactured at the Puebla plant

ABOVE & RIGHT
The seriously hardcore 3.2 litre Beetle RSi

the New Beetle, as it was named, was finally launched to the American public in 1998 before appearing a year later in Europe. A convertible was added to the range in 2003.

The New Beetle is currently available in the UK with a choice of petrol engines ranging from an economic little 1.4-litre model which produces a healthy 75bhp (that's 50% more power than the top-of-the-range Super Beetle of the 1970s) through to 2.0-litre normally aspirated and 1.8-litre turbocharged models – the latter, with 150bhp on tap, being capable of achieving acceleration from 0-62 mph in 8.7 seconds and a top speed of 126mph. For the frugally minded there is a torquey 1.9-litre turbo-diesel able to return in excess of 60 miles per gallon.

Although produced in limited numbers for a very short period of time, perhaps the ultimate New Beetle of all time was the highly acclaimed Beetle RSi. Powered by Volkswagen's glorious 3.2-litre VR6 coupled to a close ration six-speed transmission and the 4motion four-wheel drive system, its 225bhp offered acceleration from 0-62 mph in 6.4 seconds and a top speed approaching 140 mph – its thunderous soundtrack complemented superbly by the custom Remus twin-exit sports exhaust system. The suspension setup of the car, complete with rear cross-brace, was more akin to that found on the race track, as were the outsized specially manufactured 18x9 OZ Superturismo

wheels and enormous 235/40ZR-18 tyres which were tucked away under redesigned fenders that were 80mm wider than standard. Inside the cabin, carbon fibre and CNC billet aluminium were in abundance with the front seat passengers cosseted by the bright orange leather of a pair of Recaro bucket seats. The RSi may not offer the most comfortable ride of the New Beetle range but, with seriously top-end performance, it certainly is capable of giving the most exhilarating.

The New Beetle, however, is not destined to reach the heady production figures of its classic predecessor. Already, after just 12 years of production, it's set for a major change – such is the nature of the modern car industry. In recognition of its imminent demise, Volkswagen has announced another special edition model – the 2010 Volkswagen New Beetle Final Edition. Just 3,000 of these

commemorative Bugs will be produced worldwide, half of which will be coupés, half convertibles.

Following tradition, yet another special paint colour has been produced for the Final Edition – Aquarius Blue – offered in a two-tone combination with Campanella White bodywork and a white hood on the soft-top and with

a gloss black painted roof on the coupé complemented with "Final Edition" badges. Both models enjoy the benefits of 17-inch wheels, full sports suspension and a powerful 150bhp 2.5-litre I-5 motor linked to a six-speed tiptronic transmission. To finish the package, the steering wheel of each car will bear a unique edition number.

ABOVE The 2010 New Beetle Final Edition

Into the Future

A new generation of Beetle is due to hit the forecourts in spring 2011. Originally it was widely reported that Volkswagen had intentions of creating two new Beetle-named vehicles: an ultra compact city car based on its Up! concept and a larger, more traditional machine designed as a direct replacement for the current coupé and convertible models; however, it later transpired that, although VW have full intentions to realise their city-car project, it would not be branded as a Beetle.

In a departure from the existing model, the new New Beetle is set to be based on the VW Jetta platform. Providing a much wider track and increased wheelbase, it will not only offer improved ride and handling characteristics but will give designers the opportunity to significantly increase the car's interior volume. It will utilise tried and trusted suspension components from the last generation of the sporty Golf range. Engine options are yet to be confirmed but are expected to include a 170bhp 2.5-litre I-5, a torquey 2.0-litre turbo diesel and a tyre-blistering 220bhp 2.0-litre turbo injection.

Its shape is expected to be highly

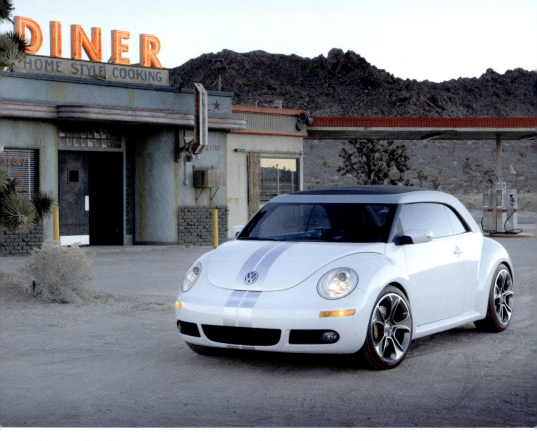

reminiscent of the Ragster concept car exhibited by Volkswagen at the 2005 Detroit International Auto Show. Although retaining the Beetle's unmistakeable shape, the new model is likely to be more angular and aggressive in design and will feature the lower and longer lines of the Ragster's "slammed" roof.

Speculation aside, one thing is for certain: the Volkswagen Beetle is set to be around for a good few years to come.

LEFT The VW Up! concept car

ABOVE The VW Ragster concept – the shape of the next generation of Beetles?

Popular Culture

Few cars, if any, could claim to have had such an impact on popular culture as has the Volkswagen Beetle.

For many years, advertising campaigns for the Beetle had been either bland – relying heavily on boring facts and statistics – or totally fantasist, making the little car out to be of limousine proportions with endless

reserves of power. But the "dull" little car from Germany soon became the antithesis of cool thanks to the efforts of American advertising agency Doyle Dane Bernbach (DDB), whose cleverly thought out "Think Small" and "Lemon" campaigns gave the Bug near human characteristics but still extolled the simple virtues of frugality and sensibility.

The Beetle, almost overnight, underwent the most incredible transformation. No longer was it seen as the mass transport of the proletariat; instead it took on a cool and rather subversive nature, becoming as much a part of 60's counterculture as it was part of the mainstream.

Andy Warhol, the bastion of all things ultra-hip and trendy, immortalised the Beetle in a 1969 work – seeing the car not as a still life but as a portrait of something living akin to his iconic Campbell's Soup Cans.

The concept of the Beetle being a living, breathing entity was taken a stage further by the Disney Studios in

"The Love Bug"; the 1968 film that first introduced us to that famous "53" car, Herbie. Such was Herbie's instant success, VW dealers across the world rushed to stock replica sets of "53" stickers and red, white and blue go-faster stripes to satisfy the thousands of owners who wanted their very own film star to play with. A movie phenomenon, everyone's favourite anthropomorphic bug has now featured in a total of five cinematic feature films, the most recent of which, "Herbie: Fully Loaded", reprised the role 36 years after the original hit the big screen.

The Beetle also makes an amusing appearance in the 1973 Woody Allen film "Sleeper". Waking from hibernation after a period of some 200 years, Allen's character, Miles Monroe, is hunted by

the authorities. Taking refuge in a cave, he discovers a familiar shape underneath a thick layer of dust – a VW Beetle that appears to have been hibernating for as long as he has. Starting on the very first turn of the key, Allen exclaims "they really built these things, didn't they?" Never a truer word said.

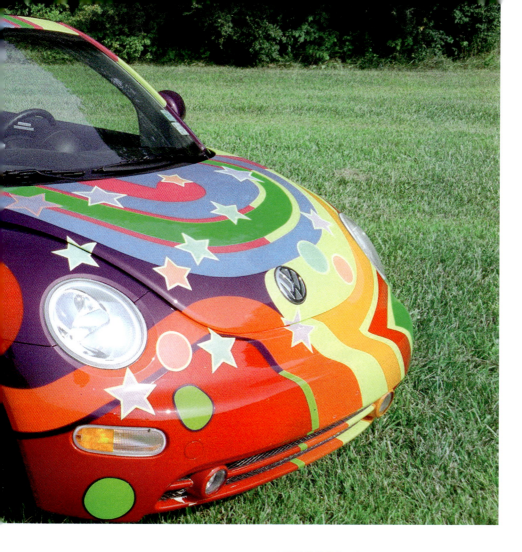

Beetlemania

The biggest and most impressive of all of the VW shows in the United Kingdom is Bug Jam. Held annually at the Santa Pod raceway in Bedfordshire, it started life as a one-day-only get-together on a warm and sunny Sunday afternoon back in July 1987. Advertised in a number of car magazines, it attracted some 3,500 visitors (although this would seem more like 35,000 from the number of people in this day and age who claimed to

have been there). Declared a resounding success, the original Bug Jam combined the best of traditional British club events with the razzmatazz and excitement of the kind of shows prevalent on the American west coast VW scene.

The show made full use of Santa

Pod's famous ¾ mile drag strip with many an air-cooled motor being pushed to the limit in a "run-what-ya-brung" straight-line dash against the clock. Always a lover of motorsport, there's no doubt that Ferdinand Porsche would have been proud even if the DayGlo

www.brickfieldautos.com

VWFestival

shorts and thumping soundtrack were not quite what he had envisaged when originally putting pen to paper to realise the Führer's dream of automotive mobilisation for the masses.

Now, bigger than ever and running over three days instead of one, the Bug Jam VW Festival holds the honour of being the largest annual V-Dub event in Europe, attracting well over 30,000 visitors.

Other essential outings for the avid air-cooled aficionado include the Heritage Bristol Volkswagen Weekend (otherwise known as the Bristol Volksfest), the London Volksfest at North Weald in Essex, Volkswagen North West at Tatton Park and the British Volkswagen Festival near Malvern. On top of those there's the plethora of VW Campervan events such as the VanFest and the legendary Run to the Sun that are more than happy to open their arms to Beetle fanatics.

The World of the Beetle

To you and me it's the Beetle or perhaps the Bug. But to the millions of Volkswagen owners the world over, this little car is known by all manner of names:

Agroga – meaning small turtle – Iraq
Beetle – United Kingdom, India, United States, Canada
Bhyagute Car – Nepal
Bimba – Israel
Bjalla – Iceland
Boblen or *Bobbelfolkevogn* – meaning the Bubble – Denmark
Bogár – Hungary
Brambar – Bulgaria
Broasca – meaning little frog – Romania
Brouk – Czech Republic
Buba – Croatia
Cepillo – meaning the brush – Dominican Republic
Chrobák – Slovakia

Coccinelle – France, Haiti
Con bo – Vietnam
Cucarachita – Guatemala, Honduras
Escarabajo – Spain, Argentina, Chile, Peru, El Salvador, Venezuela
Escarabat – Catalunya
Fakrouna – Libya
Folcika – Bosnia & Herzegovina
Folex – meaning frog – Iran
Foxi – Pakistan
Fusca – Paraguay, Brazil
Garbus – meaning hunchback – Poland
Hroš – Slovenia
Ji Ké Chóng – China
Jin-guei che – Taiwan
Kabuto-mushi – Japan
Käfer – Germany, Switzerland, Austria
Kaplumba a – Turkey
Kever – Netherlands
Kifuu – Kenya
Kodok – meaning frog – Indonesia
Kotseng Kuba – meaning hunchback car

– Philippines
Kuplavolkkari – Finland
Maggiolino – Italy
Mgongo wa Chura – meaning frog back
– Swahili
Mwendo wa Kobe – meaning tortoise
speed – Swahili
Peta – meaning turtle – Bolivia
Pichirilo – Ecuador
Poncho – Chile

Põrnikas – Estonia
Pulga – meaning flea – Colombia
Rod Tao – meaning turtle car – Thailand
Scathari – Greece
Scoro-Scoro – Namibia
Vabalas – Lithuania
Vocho – Mexico, Costa Rica
Volky – Puerto Rico
Volla – South Africa
Zhuk – Russia

ALSO AVAILABLE IN THE LITTLE BOOK SERIES

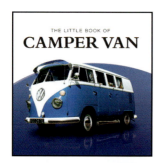

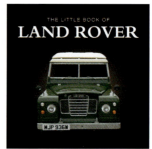

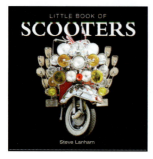

ALSO AVAILABLE IN THE LITTLE BOOK SERIES

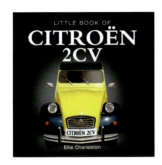

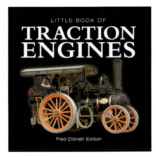

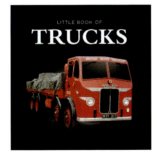

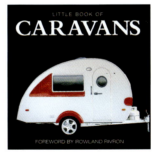

**The pictures in this book were provided
courtesy of the following:**

GETTY IMAGES
101 Bayham Street, London NW1 0AG

MOTORING PICTURE LIBRARY
www.motoringpicturelibrary.com

Design and artwork by Scott Giarnese

Published by G2 Entertainment Limited

Publishers Jules Gammond and Edward Adams

Written by Jon Stroud